Hindi/Urdu phrasebook

lonely planet

Parvez Dewan

Hindi/Urdu Phrasebook

Published by
Lonely Planet Publications
Head Office: PO Box 88, South Yarra, Victoria 3141, Australia
US Office: PO Box 2001A, Berkeley, CA 94702, USA

Printed by
Colorcraft, Hong Kong

Thanks from the publisher to
Mrs Sudhā Joshi & Adrian McNeil, Melbourne

Dedicated to
My Gurus: S Gian Singh, Rita Mukherjee & Anees Jung

First published
May 1988

Editor	Susan Mitra
Design, cover design & illustrations	Greg Herriman
Typesetting	Ann Jeffree

National Library of Australia Cataloguing in Publication Data

Dewan, Parvez
Hindi/Urdu phrasebook
ISBN 0 86442 004 8.
1. Hindi language - Conversation and phrase books - English.
2. Urdu language - Conversation and phrase books - English. I Title.
(Series: Language survival kit).

491'.4383'421

Contents

Introduction

India and Pakistan are countries where many languages are spoken. In the case of India, the north Indian languages (Hindi, Bengali, Marathi, etc) belong to a different language family from the languages spoken in the south (Tamil, Telugu, etc). Hindi and Urdu are the most widely understood languages in India and Pakistan.

As far as the spoken languages are concerned, there is very little difference between Hindi and Urdu. The sentence structure, the grammar, the sound system, just about everything is identical. However, just as the English people have their trunk-calls, lifts and colours, and Americans have long-distance calls, elevators and colors – the same kinds of differences are found between Hindi and Urdu.

One of the main differences between Hindi and Urdu is that they have different parent languages. Hindi is a Sanskrit-based language whereas Urdu draws from the Persian and Arabic languages. Another difference is that Hindi is written in the Devanagari script which has come from Sanskrit and Urdu is written in the Arabic script. Nowadays though, Hindi and Urdu share a large common vocabulary.

Wherever possible words common to both Hindi and Urdu have been used in this phrasebook. This has meant that at times a whole phrase (common to both) instead of a single word (exclusive to either) has been listed. Sometimes there is no option but to use a word which is exclusive to one, in such cases this phrasebook indicates the pure Hindi word with an (H) and the Urdu word with a (U). For example, the Hindi word for television is *dūrdarshan* (literally, 'view from afar') but the Urdu word for television is *ṭélīvizyon*. In other cases although Hindi and Urdu have separate words, one word may be more commonly understood than the other. In these cases the word will be marked with (mc) which indicates that it is in more common usage. A simple rule of thumb would be to use the Hindi word in India and Nepal and the Urdu word in Pakistan, except in the Indian state of Jammu & Kashmir where Urdu is more popular than Hindi because of the large Muslim population.

If you are on a five-star luxury vacation and do not intend to go anywhere on your own, most of the people you'll meet will speak English. Away from that scene, your attempts to speak the language will be appreciated and should make your travels much easier and hopefully more enjoyable.

Pronunciation

Hindi/Urdu and English all belong to the same language family – Indo-European – which means that they have many similarities, however, there are some sounds in Hindi/Urdu which are not found in English.

Vowels

a	as the 'u' in	'cup'
i	as the 'i' in	'in'
e	as the 'e' in	'get'
u	as the 'u' in	'put'

There are also long vowel sounds:

ā	as the 'a' in	'father'
ī	as the 'e' in	'eat'
ai	as the 'a' in	'add'
ū	as the 'o' in	'do'
o	as the 'oa' in	'coal'
au	as the 'ow' in	'how'
é	as the 'ay' in	'day'

Consonants

b	as the 'b' in	'bear'
ch	as the 'ch' in	'church'
d	as the 'd' in	'dear'
f	as the 'f' in	'forgive'
g	as the 'g' in	'give' not in 'gin'
j	as the 'j' in	'jam'
k	as the 'k' in	'skip'

kh	as the 'k' in	'kite'
ḳh	as the 'ch' in	*ich* (German)
l	as the 'l' in	'light'
m	as the 'm' in	'man'
n	as the 'n' in	'noon'
ñ	as the 'n' in	*pardon* (French)
ng	as the 'ng' in	'song'
p	as the 'p' in	'spot'
ph	as the 'p' in	'pot'
r	as the 'r' in	'rat'
s	as the 's' in	'same'
sh	as the 's' in	'sugar'
t	as the 't' in	'stop'
th	as the 't' in	'top'
v	as the 'v' in	'veil'
w	as the 'w' in	'wave'
y	as the 'y' in	'yes'
z	as the 'z' in	'zero'

Other Consonants

Now for the sounds that are not to be found in English. Most of these sounds are the aspirated and retroflex consonants. If you find these sounds difficult settle for the nearest equivalent in the English language.

Aspiration

An example of aspiration in English is the difference between the 't' in 'stop' and 'top'. If you put your hand to your mouth and pronounce these words you will feel the air as you say 'top' but not when you say 'stop'. Aspiration in Hindi/Urdu is more forceful and more important than it is in English because it changes the meanings of words.

aspirated consonant	as in	meaning	nearest English equivalent
bh	*bhikārī*	beggar	b
chh	*achchha*	good, OK	ch
dh	*dhan*	wealth	dh (as in *dharma*)
gh	*ghar*	house	g
jh	*jhaṇḍā*	flag	j
kh	*khānā*	food	k
ph	*phal*	fruit	f
th	*thailā*	bag	th

Retroflex consonants

The retroflex sound is made by touching the back of the roof of your mouth with your tongue as you pronounce the consonant. Curl your tongue like a hooked finger to make these sounds. This sound is applicable to the letters 't' and 'd'. Try saying 't' several times, moving your tongue further back along the roof of your mouth each time.

retroflex consonant	as in	meaning	nearest English equivalent
ḍ	*ḍar*	fear	d
ḍh	*ḍhér*	a heap	d
ṭ	*ṭamāṭar*	tomato	t
ṭh	*ṭhanḍā*	cold	t
ṛ	*gāṛī*	vehicle	r or d
ṛh	*sīṛhī*	ladder	r or d

The unaspirated Arabic/Persian consonants 'g' and 'k' are pronounced as in English only further back in the throat.

g	*gadar*	mutiny	g
q	*qarz*	debt	k

And finally:
r In Hindi/Urdu **r** is invariably pronounced, if not trilled.

Abbreviations used in this Book

(H) – Hindi
(U) – Urdu
(mc) – more common
(m) – masculine
(f) – feminine
(sing) – singular
(pl) – plural
(v) – verb
(n) – noun
(adj) – adjective

Grammar

Word Order

In simple sentences the order in which words occur usually fit into the following pattern: subject-object-verb. For example:

The pen is on the table. *kalam méz par hai*
(pen table on is)

The articles 'the', 'a', or 'an' are not used in Hindi/Urdu. Expressions such as 'there is' can be implied by inversing the order of the sentence but a Hindi/Urdu speaker would generally just say 'pen is'. For example:

There is a pen on the table. *méz par kalam hai*

To negate a statement a negative such as *nahīñ* is generally placed before the verb. For example:

The pen isn't on the table. *kalam méz par nahīñ hai*

Other objects and adverbial expressions can be placed between the subject and verb in a less fixed order. Expressions of time most often appear at the beginning of a sentence and precede expressions of place. For example:

The pen isn't on the table now. *ab kalam méz par nahīñ hai*
The pen is now on the table in that room *ab us kamré méñ kalam méz par hai*

Interrogative pronouns and adverbs, such as *kahāñ* and *kyā*, usually appear after the subject. For example:

Where is the pen?	*kalam kahāñ hai?*
What is this?	*yah kyā hai?*

Nouns

There are two genders in Hindi/Urdu, male and female. Each noun is attributed with one of these genders. There is no absolute way of determining a noun's gender other than through memorising it. However, as a very general rule, Hindi/Urdu nouns that end in the vowel *a* are usually masculine, while nouns that end in the vowel *i* are usually feminine. For example:

masculine	**feminine**
laṛkā - boy	*laṛkī* - girl
kélā - banana	*gāṛī* - vehicle
kamrā - room	*kursī* - chair

Hindi/Urdu nouns can be either singular or plural. There are only two cases which need to be distinguished - direct and oblique. The direct form of a noun usually denotes sentence subjects or direct objects, whilst the oblique form is used when a postposition follows the noun.

The way a noun is declined from direct to oblique depends on whether it is masculine or feminine, singular or plural. The following is an example of how masculine and feminine nouns regularly decline.

masculine

singular direct	*laṛkā* - boy

singular oblique	*laṛké* as in *laṛké ko* – to the boy
plural direct	*laṛké* – boys
plural oblique	*laṛkoñ* as in *laṛkoñ ko* – to the boys

feminine

singular direct	*laṛkī* – girl
singular oblique	*laṛkī* – girl (does not decline)
plural direct	*laṛkiyāñ* – girls
plural oblique	*laṛkiyoñ* as in *laṛkiyoñ ko* – to the girls

There are many irregularities in noun declension. The best way to learn the various exceptions to the rules is through careful listening and practise.

Adjectives

In most cases an adjective appears before the noun it modifies, the exception being when a predicative adjective is used. The adjective often changes form so as to agree with the gender and number of the noun that it modifies, as the examples show.

Singular direct nouns

masculine	*chotā kamrā*	– small room
feminine	*chotī kursī*	– small chair

Plural direct nouns

masculine	*choté kamré*	– small rooms
feminine	*chotī kursiyāñ*	– small chairs

Feminine adjectives do not have plural forms, so they do not change to agree with plural direct nouns. They are also unaffected when used to describe singular or plural oblique nouns.

Singular oblique nouns

choṭī kursī ko	– to the small chair
choṭī kursiyoṅ ko	– to the small chairs

Only adjectives ending in *ā* change when preceding a noun – other adjectives remain unchanged. Some of the more common adjectives which do not change are:

many, very	*bahut*
bad	*kharāb*
clean	*sāf*
beautiful	*sundar*

As with English, several adjectives can also be combined together to modify a single noun:

a very bad room	*bahut kharāb kamrā*

Personal Pronouns

In Hindi/Urdu, pronouns reflect the comparative social and kinship positions between the speaker and the person referred to. This is achieved through the three levels of address inherent in the hierarchy of second and third person pronouns. The safest and most polite form of address to use is *āp*. When addressing friends who are about the same age as you, it is generally OK to address them as *tum* but as a rule never call anyone *tū*.

I	*maiñ*
we	*ham*
you (intimate)	*tū*
you (familiar)	*tum*
you	*āp*
he, she, it (familiar)	*wah*
he, she, (formal & near person)	*yé*
he, she, (formal & away from person)	*vé/woh*
they (near person)	*yé, yé log* (literally, these people)
they (away from person)	*vé, vé log*

Possessive Pronouns

my	*mérā*
our	*hamarā*
your (intimate)	*térā*
your (familiar)	*tumharā*
your (formal)	*āpkā*
his, hers, its (familiar)	*uskā*
his, hers (formal & near person)	*inkā*
his, hers (formal & away from person)	*unkā*
theirs (near person)	*inkā*
theirs (away from person)	*unkā*

The possessive pronouns are in masculine agreement form. If the noun that follows the possessive pronoun is feminine then the pronouns would change according to the gender of the noun not the possessor. For example:

my chair	*mérī kursī*
your chair	*āpkī kursī*

Is/Are

This is the most commonly used verb in Hindi/Urdu and, as in English, it is also the verb that varies most from the standard pattern. Therefore it is necessary to memorise the different forms of *honā*. The following shows how *honā* agrees with personal pronouns.

I am	*maiñ .... hūñ*
You are	*tum .... ho*
You are	*āp .... haiñ*
He/she/it is	*vah .... hai*
This is	*yah .... hai*
They are	*vé/woh .... haiñ*

Postpositions

Postpositions function in Hindi/Urdu in much the same way that prepositions are used in English. They invariably follow the noun or pronoun which appears in oblique form. They may be simple or compound. The most common postpositions are:

ko	generally is used as the English preposition 'to'
kā	the possessive 'of', but changes to *kī* if the noun possessed is feminine, or *ké* if masculine plural
né	past tense marker
méñ	in, among

par	on
ké pās	near to
tak	up to, until
sé	from, through, by, then
ké sāth	with
ké liyé	for
ké binā	without

Verbs

The two basic structural components of Hindi/Urdu verbs are the verb stem and formative suffixes. These suffixes are added to the stem of the verb in order to indicate the agreement of tense, gender and number, with the subject of the sentence. For example, the active or transitive verb 'to see' is *dékhnā*. The stem can be formed by dropping *nā* from this infinitive form. The stem therefore is *dékh*. Suffixes added to the stem conjugate the verb in the following way:

person	past	future	present
1st (*maiñ*)	*dékhā* (m)	*dékhuñgā* (m)	*dékhtā* (m)
	dékhī (f)	*dékhuñgī* (f)	*dékhtī* (f)
2nd (*āp*)	*dékhé* (m)	*dékhéñgé* (m)	*dékhté* (m)
	dékhī (f)	*dékhéñgī* (f)	*dékhtī* (f)

3rd person (*yé/vé/woh*) is the same as 2nd person *āp*

Generally this is the pattern by which Hindi/Urdu verbs are conjugated although in Hindi/Urdu there are many exceptions to this rule as certain verbs conjugate in irregular ways.

Passive verbs - intransitive

Any verb that does not have a direct object is intransitive. For example, in Hindi/Urdu, hunger is expressed as a state of being that affects an individual. It is not expressed in the direct way in which we say in English, 'I'm hungry' but literally as 'hunger is felt by me' – *mujhé bhūkh lagī hai*. Similarly, any verb that cannot have a direct object is also intransitive, for example:

to come	*ānā*
to go	*jānā*
to be	*honā*
to arrive	*pahuñchanā*
to get up	*uṭhanā*
to sleep	*sonā*

Question Construction

As with English, there are two ways of forming a question in Hindi/Urdu. One way is to use an interrogative word such as 'where', 'why', 'how', etc, and the other is by turning a statement into a question by an inflexion of the voice.

Interrogative words

what	*kyā*
who	*kaun*
where	*kahāñ*
when	*kab*
how many/much	*kitnā*
why	*kyoñ*
whose	*kiskā*
which one	*kaun sā*

What is this?	*yah kyā hai?*
Who is this?	*yah kaun hai?*
Where is the hotel?	*hotel kahāñ hai?*
When did you come?	*āp kab āyé?*
How much?	*kitnā hai?*
Whose is this?	*yah kiskā hai?*
Which one is this?	*yah kaun sā hai?*

Construction Expressing to Want & Need

Positive construction

I want tea. *mujhé chāy chahiyé*

Negative construction

I don't want tea. *mujhé chāy nahīñ chahiyé*

With interrogative words

Where do you want to go? *āp kahāñ jānā chahté haiñ?*

Question formation

Do you want tea? *kyā āpko chāy chahiyé?*

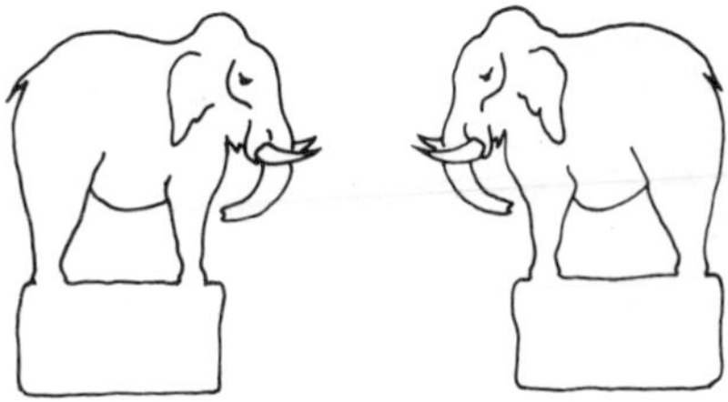

Greetings & Civilities

Greetings

There are no good mornings or good evenings in Hindi/Urdu, but nonetheless, there are traditional greetings.

Hindus on meeting each other say *namasté*, literally, 'I bow to thee' and fold their palms together.

Muslims greet each other by saying *salām alékum*, literally, 'peace be on you'. The reply is either the same words, or *vālékum as salām* – 'and also on you'.

Goodbyes

Hindus say *namasté* and Muslims say *khudā hāfiz*, literally, 'may God protect you' or, poetically, *shabbā khair* 'good night'.

Some Useful Phrases

How are you?
  āp kaisé haiñ?
Very well, thank you.
  bahut achchhé shukriyā
Thank you.
  shukriyā
Excuse me. (literally, 'forgive me')
  māf kījiyé
Thank you very much.
  bahut, bahut shukriyā
You're welcome (literally, 'It doesn't matter')
  koī bāt nahīñ

Forms of Address

If you want to address a stranger, the safest form of address in the Hindi/Urdu areas (including Bangladesh) would be *janāb* which means 'sir'.

Jī is a very polite expression which has no meaning in particular but is used often in everyday speech. It can be used as 'yes' in reply to a question and is often said after a person's name, for example, *Sudhājī* or *Pandéjī*. South Indians, who speak little Hindi/Urdu, use *sār* (sir) instead of *jī* when addressing men. Hence *Venkat-sār, Pandé-sār*, and so on.

Small Talk

Many words used in Hindi/Urdu will be familiar to English-speakers as many words have come from English in the first place. When you are chatting with people, don't hesitate to use an English word if you're stuck; the word may very well be understood.

When you are addressing people it is best to use *āp* rather than any other second person (you) pronoun.

About Yourself

My name is ....
mérā nām .... hai
What is your name?
āpkā nām kyā hai?
Where do you come from?
āp kahāñ ké rehné vālé haiñ? (m)
āp kahāñ kī rehné vālī haiñ? (f)

I live in	*maiñ .... méñ rehtā hūñ* (m) *maiñ .... méñ rehtī hūñ* (f)
Australia	*osṭréliyā*
Canada	*kainaḍā*
China	*chīn*
Egypt	*misr* (H)
England	*inglainḍ*
Greece	*yunān* or *grīs*

Japan	*jāpān*
Russia	*rūs*
USA	*amrīkā*

I am a/an	*maiñ .... hūñ*
American	*amrīkan*
British	*angréz*

What is your occupation?
āp kyā kām karté haiñ?

I am a/an	*maiñ .... hūñ*
actor	*aikṭar*
actress	*aikṭrés*
builder	*bilḍar*
doctor	*ḍokṭar*
journalist	*patrakār* (H) *akhbār nabīs*
lawyer	*vakīl*
musician	*myūzishan*
student	*paṛh rahā hūñ* (m) *paṛh rahī hūñ* (f)
teacher	*tīchar*

What is your religion?
āpkā dharm kyā hai? (H)
āpkā mazhab kyā hai? (U)

I am	*maiñ .... hūñ*
Hindu	*hindū*
Muslim	*mussalmān*
Christian	*īsāī*
Jewish	*yahūdī*
Buddhist	*bauddh dharm kā* (m) *bauddh dharm kī* (f)

Some Useful Phrases

How's it going?
kaisā chal rahā hai?
Fine/Well.
ṭhīk ṭhāk
Can you help me?
kyā āp mérī madad kar sakté haiñ?
I am looking for ....
maiñ .... ko ḍhūñḍh rahā hūñ (m)
maiñ .... ko ḍhūñḍh rahī hūñ (f)
How old are you?
āpkī umr kyā hai?
I'm .... years old.
mérī umr .... sāl hai
I don't understand.
mérī samajh méñ nahīñ āyā
Can you speak English?
kyā āp angrézī bol sakté haiñ? (m)
kyā āp angrézī bol saktī haiñ? (f)
Do you understand English?
kyā āp angrézi samajhté haiñ? (m)
kyā āp angrézi samajhtī haiñ? (f)
I speak very little Hindi.
maiñ bahut kam hindī jāntā hūñ (m)
maiñ bahut kam hindī jāntī hūñ (f)
Please speak a little slower?
zarā āhistā bol sakté haiñ? (m)
zarā āhistā bol saktī haiñ? (f)
Where do you live?
āp kahāñ rehté haiñ? (m)
āp kahāñ rehtī haiñ? (f)

Family

It is perfectly normal to address people with kinship terms according to their age in relation to yours. To someone who is about your age you could use brother or sister, and to someone who is quite a bit older you could call them mother or father.

	Hindu	**Muslim**	**religion-neutral**
father	*pitājī*	*vālid sāb*	
mother	*mātājī*	*vālidā sāhibā*	
older brother	*bhaīyā*	*bhāī*	*bhāī*
older sister	*dīdī*	*āpā*	*behin*
brother			*bhāī*
sister			*behin*
son			*béṭā*
daughter			*béṭī*
husband	*pati*	*khāvand*	
wife			*bībī/bīvī*

Some useful phrases

Are you married?
kyā āp kī shādī ho chukī hai?
How many brothers (children) do you have?
āp ké kitné bhāī (bachché) haiñ?
How many sisters do you have?
āp kī kitnī behin haiñ?

Feelings

I'm	*mujhé .... hai*
cold	*ṭhanḍ lag rahī*
drunk	*nashā chaṛh gayā*

hot	*garmī lag rahī*
hungry	*bhūkh lagī*
not hungry	*bhūkh nahīñ*
scared	*ḍar lag rahā*
sleepy	*nīñd lag rahī*
not sleepy	*nīñd nahīñ ā rahī*
thirsty	*pyās lag rahī*

Accommodation

The Indian subcontinent boasts of some of the world's finest hotels. Some of these were previously palaces which have now been converted into luxury hotels. In India the traditional places to stay are the *sarāya* (serai), the Hindu *dharamshālā* (the house of religion) and the Sikh *gurudwārā* (the guru's doorstep).

While serais and *dharamshālās* aren't so much in evidence these days, *gurudwārās* continue to house and feed people, irrespective of religion or nationality.

Some Useful Phrases

Is there a place to stay (nearby)?
(ās pās koī) rehné kī jagā hai?
A good place.
koī achchhī sī jagā
Anything will do.
kuchh bhī chalégā
Are there rooms available?
koī kamrā khālī hai?
Can I sleep here?
kyā maiñ yahāñ so saktā hūñ? (m)
kyā maiñ yahāñ so saktī hūñ? (f)
What is the rent for a day?
ék din kā kyā kirāyā hai?
Do you have a cheaper room?
is sé sastā kamrā hai?
Is a bathroom attached?
sāth méñ bāthrūm hai?

Does it have hot water?
us méñ garam pānī hai?
Can I see the room?
kyā maiñ kamrā dékh saktā hūñ? (m)
kyā maiñ kamrā dékh saktī hūñ? (f)
Do you have any other rooms?
kyā āp ké pās aur koī kamrā hai?
Can you lower the rate?
kyā āp kirāyā kam kar sakté haiñ?
If the hotel owner is female, you say:
kyā āp kirāyā kam kar saktī haiñ?
Can you lower it further?
kuchh aur kam kar sakté haiñ?
I/we'll stay (two nights).
ham (do rāt) rahéñgé
Where can I wash my clothes?
kapṛé kahāñ dho saktā hūñ? (m)
kapṛé kahāñ dho saktī hūñ? (f)
Can I leave my (bag) here?
apnā (jholā) yahāñ chhoṛ saktā hūñ? (m)
apnā (jholā) yahāñ chhoṛ saktī hūñ? (f)
I'll return in (two weeks).
maiñ (do haftoñ) méñ vāpis ā jahuñgā (m)
maiñ (do haftoñ) méñ vāpis ā jahuñgī (f)

Where is the ....?	.... *kahāñ hai?*
hotel	*hoṭal*
mosque	*masjid*
restaurant	*khāné kī jagā* or *resṭūrent*
shop	*dukān*
temple	*mandir*

Do you have a ....?	*āp ké pās .... hai?*
room	*ék kamrā*
bathroom	*bāthrūm; gusalkhānā*
bed	*bistarā* or *bistar*
ordinary room	*sādā kamrā*
air-conditioned room	*éyar kondishonḍ kamrā*
Is there ....?	*........ hai?*
a telephone	*ṭélifon*
laundry service	*kapṛé dhoné wālā* or *dhobī*
hot water	*garam pānī*
breakfast	*nāshtā* or *subah kā nāshtā*
How much is ....?	*........ ké kitné paisé lagéñgé?*
it per night	*ék rāt*
a cheaper room	*is sé sasté kamré*
the bill	*bil*
the meal	*khāné* (H & U)
	bhojan (H)
one week's rent	*ék hafté*
one month's rent	*ék mahīné*

How much?
kitnā hai?
All these things are mine.
yé sab chīzéñ mérī haiñ
This room is too big.
yé kamrā bahut baṛā hai
This room is too small.
yé kamrā bahut chhoṭā hai
Please bring it as soon as you can.
zarā jaldī lāyéñ

Some Useful Words

accommodation	*rehné kī jagā*
address	*patā*
arrival	*ānā* (H & U); *āgaman* (H)
bathe	*nahānā*
bedroom	*soné kā kamrā* or *beḍrūm*
blanket	*kambal*
box	*baks*
bulb	*balb*
clean	*sāf*
cost (n)	*kīmat*
crowded (with people)	*(logoñ sé) bharā huā*
dinner	*rāt kā khānā*
dirty	*gandā*
electric	*bijlī wālā*
elevator	*lifṭ*
exit (n)	*bāhar kā darvāzā*
fan	*pankhā*
food	*khānā*
lock	*tālā*
mosquito net	*masharī*
pillow	*sirhānā* or *takīyā*
roof/ceiling	*chhat*
soiled	*mailā*
sheet	*chādar*
suitcase	*sūṭkés; baksā*

Getting Around

Good, bad or indifferent, clean or dirty, punctual or not, the public transport in the subcontinent (buses, trains, steamers - everything except the airlines) is cheap. Many taxis do not use their meters which means that it is important for you to establish the price before you go. Taxi drivers and rickshaw-wallas are notorious for not having any small change on them, so try to keep some for these occasions.

In India and Bangladesh it is a good idea to book in advance if travelling long distance by train. When it comes to road journeys, one can only reserve tickets on deluxe buses. Aeroplane tickets for internal travel are very difficult to get at short notice in India.

Where is the ....?	.... *kahāñ hai?*
station	*sṭéshan*
bus stop	*bas sṭāp*
dining car	*ḍāining kār*
ticket office	*ṭīkaṭ āphis*
airport	*éyarporṭ*
What .... is this?	*yé kaun sī .... hai?*
street	*saṛak*
city	*shehar*
When will the .... leave?	.... *kab jāégī?*
bus	*bas*
next bus	*aglī bas*

Trains are sometimes called *gāṛī* (which is also the generic term for all vehicles, including animal powered) or *rél gāṛī*.

I would like ...	*maiñ ... pasand karūñgā* (m)
	maiñ ... pasand karūñgī (f)
a sleeper	*slīpar*
berth	*barth*
upper	*ūpar wālā*
lower	*nīché wālā*
two tickets to ...	*... ke liyé do ṭikaṭ*

Some Useful Words

bicycle	*sāikal*
boat	*kishtī*
bridge	*pul*
car	*gāṛī* (or *moṭar gāṛī* or *kār*)
coast	*kinārā* (H & U); *sāhil* (U)
crowd	*bhīṛ*
daily	*rozānā*
early (quickly)	*jaldī*
early in the morning	*subah savéré*
hire (v)	*kirāyé pé lénā*
petrol	*peṭrol* (or *tél*)
road	*saṛak*
taxi	*ṭaiksi*
ticket	*ṭikaṭ*

Directions

how far?	*kitnā dūr?*
right	*dāhinā* or *dāéñ*

left	*bāéñ*
north	*uttar* (H); *shumāl* (U)
south	*dakshin* (H & U); *junūb* (U)
east	*pūrab* (H); *mashriq* (U)
west	*pashchim* (H); *maghrib* (U)

Some Useful Phrases

Is someone sitting here?
kyā yahāñ koī baiṭhā huā hai?
Someone is sitting here.
yahāñ koī baiṭhā huā hai
May I/we sit here?
kyā ham yahāñ baiṭh sakté haiñ?
Can I/we (put) my/our bag here?
kyā ham apnā baig yahāñ (rakh) sakté haiñ?
Can you wait for me?
āp mérā intézār kar sakté haiñ?
How many (kilometres)?
kitné (kilomīṭar)?
I am looking for ....
maiñ .... ko ḍhūñḍh rahā hūñ (m)
maiñ .... ko ḍhūñḍh rahī hūñ (f)
Where are you going?
āp kahāñ jā rahé haiñ?
I want to go to ....
maiñ .... jānā chāhtā hūñ (m)
maiñ .... jānā chāhtī hūñ (f)
How much will it cost to go to ....
.... jāné ké liyé kitnā paisā lagégā?
Can you wait here?
kyā āp yahāñ intézār kar sakté haiñ?

Drive slowly please.
zarā āhistā chalāiyé
I will get out here.
maiñ yahāñ utrūñgā (m)
maiñ yahāñ utrūñgī (f)
Which bus goes to ....?
.... *kaun sī bas jātī hai?*
Does this bus go to ....?
kyā yé bas .... jātī hai?
What's the fare?
kirāyā kitnā hai?
Where can one catch the bus to ....?
.... *jāné wālī bas kahāñ milégī?*
When will the bus leave?
bas kab chalégī?
How many buses per day are there to ....?
.... *ko din méñ kitnī baséñ jātī haiñ?*
What time does the bus reach ....?
bas .... kitné bajé pahuñchégī?
When the bus reaches .... please tell me.
jab bas .... pahuñché to mujhé batāiyégā
Can I/we stop over in ....?
kyā ham .... méñ ṭheher sakté haiñ?
Is .... far from here?
kyā .... yahāñ sé dūr hai?
Is .... nearby?
kyā .... nazdīk hai?
Stop here.
yahāñ rukiyégā

Around Town

Where is the ....?	.... *kahāṅ hai?*
bank	*baink*
barber	*nāī*
market	*bāzār*
church	*girjā ghar*
mosque	*masjid*
temple - Hindu	*mandir*
- Sikh	*gurudwārā*
- Jain	*jain mandir*
How far is the ....?	.... *kitnī dūr hai?*
factory	*faikṭarī; kārkhānā*
Indian laundry	*dhobī kī dukān*
western-style laundry	*ḍrāī klīnar*
I'm looking for the	*maiṅ* .... *ḍhūṅḍh rahā hūṅ*
museum	*myūzīyam* or *ajāyab ghar*
park	*pārk* or *bāg* (gardens)
cinema	*sinémā*

When does it open?
vo kab khultā hai?
When does it close?
vo kab band hotā hai?

Some Useful Words

lawyer	*vakīl*
beggar	*bhikhārī*

capital	*rājdhānī*
fortune-teller	*jyotishī*
map	*nakshā*
movie	*pikchar*
school (western-style)	*skūl*
shop	*dukān*
village	*gāoñ*
zoo	*chiṛiya ghar*

At the Post Office

Where is the post office?
ḍāk khānā kahāñ hai?
What does it cost to send a ....?
ék .... bhéjné ké liyé kitné paisé lagéñgé?
postcard, aerogramme, etc, as in English.

May I have	*mujhé .... chāhiyé*
stamps (postal)	*ḍāk ṭikaṭ*
envelope	*lifāfā*
insurance	*bīmā*
receipt	*rasīd*

Some useful phrases

This letter is going to the USA.
yé chiṭṭhī amrīkā ké liyé hai
How much is it to send this letter to England?
is chiṭṭhī ko inglainḍ bhéjné méñ kitné paisé lagéñgé?
I would like (five) aerogrammes, please.
mujhé (pāñch) érogrām chāhiyé, jī
I want to send this package by airmail.
maiñ is pārsal ko éyarmél sé bhéjnā chāhtā hūñ (m)
maiñ is pārsal ko éyarmél sé bhéjna chāhtī hūñ (f)

I (need/want) a receipt.
mujhé rasīd (ki zurūrat hai/chāhiyé)
I want to insure/register this parcel.
maiñ is pārsal ko inshor/rajisṭar karānā chāhtā hūñ
What will it cost?
kitné paisé lagéñgé?
I want three 50 paise stamps, please.
mujhé tīn pachās paisé ke ṭikaṭ chāhiyé jī
How much per word?
har lafz (U)/shabd (H) ké liyé kitnā?
Have you received any mail for ....?
.... ké liyé koī chiṭṭhi āī hai?

At the Bank

When changing money, ask the teller to give you a range of denominations as having all large notes can be a hassle.

Where is the bank?
baink kahāñ hai?

I want to change	*maiñ .... badalnā chāhtā hūñ*
money	*paisé*
US dollars	*amrīkan ḍolar*
British pounds	*angrézī paunḍ*

What is the exchange rate for ....?	*........ kā ikschénj réṭ kyā hai?*
German marks	*jarmanī ké mārk*
Australian dollars	*osṭréliyā ké ḍolar*

Some useful phrases

I need to change money.
mujhé paisé badalné ki zurūrat hai
Can I change money here?
kyā yahāñ paisé badlé jā sakté haiñ?
I need to cash this cheque.
maiñ is chek ko kaish karānā chāhtā hūñ
Can I exchange this bill (note) for smaller change?
kyā āp is noṭ ké badlé chénj dé sakté haiñ?

Some useful words

money	*paisé*
coins	*sikké*
notes	*noṭ*

Police

police station	*thānā*
thief	*chor*
help!	*bachāo!*

I have been robbed.
mérī chorī ho gaī hai
I didn't do anything.
maiñné kuchh nahīñ kiyā
It is not mine.
vo mérā nahīñ hai

In the Country

Weather

weather	*mausam*
climate	*ābohavā* (literally, water & air)
breeze	*havā; sabu* (morning breeze)
dusty wind	*dhūl bharī havā*
fog	*kohrā*
mist	*dhundh*
lightning	*bijlī*
very hot	*bahut garam*
cool weather	*ṭhanḍā mausam*

Some useful phrases

How's the weather?
mausam kaisā hai?
It is cold?
ṭhanḍā hai?
Is it going to rain?
kyā bārish hogī?
The weather is nice today.
āj mausam achchhā hai.

Seasons

summer	*garmī*
winter	*sardī*
spring	*bahār; basant*
autumn	*patjhaṛ*
the monsoons	*sāwan; barsāt*

Some Useful Phrases

How far is the	.... *kitnī dūr hai?*
sea-shore	*samundar kā kinārā*
temple	*mandir*
mosque	*masjid*
camp (n)	*kaimp*
cave	*gufā*
hill	*pahāṛ*
Where is the ....?	.... *kahāñ hai?*
field	*khét*
lake	*tālāb*
ocean	*samundar*
river	*nadī, dariyā*
waterfall	*jharnā* (H & U) *ābshār* (U)
main road	*mén rod*
Is there (any) ....?	.... *hai?*
rope	*rassī*
snow, ice	*barf*
stone	*patthar*
mud	*kīchaṛ*
water	*pānī*

Animals

ant	*chyūñṭī*
bee	*shehed ki makkhī; madhumakkhī*
bird	*chiṛiyā*
buffalo	*bhaiñs*
butterflies	*titliyāñ*
calf	*bachhṛā*

chameleon	*girgiṭ*
cobra	*nāg*
cockroach	*khaṭmal*
cow	*gāy*
crocodile	*magar-machchh*
deer	*hiran*
dog	*kuttā*
duck	*battakh*
elephant	*hāthī*
fish (generic)	*machhlī*
a fly (n)	*makkhī*
frog	*méñḍhak*
horse	*ghoṛā*
insect (generic)	*kīṛā*
lion	*shér*
lizard	*chhipkalī*
mosquito	*machchhar*
rabbit	*khargosh*
snake	*sāñp*
tiger	*chītā*

Some Useful Words

accident (generic)	*aiksiḍenṭ*
collision	*ṭakkar*
agriculture	*khéti bārī* (colloquial)
ash(es)	*rākh*
bait (worm)	*chārā; kéñchuā*
bamboo	*bāñs*
bark (tree)	*péṛ kī chhāl*
betel	*pān*
betel nut	*supārī*
bridge	*pul*

clam (shell)	*sīpī*
climb (v)	*chaṛho, chaṛhiyé* (polite)
climb (ascent) (n)	*chaṛhān*
cloud	*bādal*
coconut	*nāriyal*
conch	*shañkh*
corn	*makkā*
countryside	*déhāt*
dam	*ḍaim*
danger	*khatarā*
dust	*dhūl; gardā*
earthquake	*bhūchāl* (H); *zalzalā* (U)
farmer	*kisān*
fisherman	*machhuārā*
ground	*zamīn*
earth	*dhartī* (H)
hunt	*shikār*
hut	*jhoñpaṛā*
leaf	*pattā*
lotus	*kamal*
nature	*qudrat* (U, mc); *prakriti* (H)
nest	*ghoñsalā*
poison	*zeher*
poisonous	*zehrīlā*

Trekking

The tallest mountains and the most exciting treks in the world are in South Asia, mostly along the northern Himalayan belt, however, not all of these are Hindi/Urdu speaking areas. Still, some Hindi/Urdu is understood by many of the people in northern Pakistan, Ladakh, Himachal Pradesh, northern Uttar Pradesh, Bihar and even Nepal. Even in the hills of Bengal the language will help you.

Unless you take a route not popular with other trekkers, you are unlikely to face any serious problems by the way of porters, equipment, language or food. The biggest problem will be the quality of drinking water.

In the Buddhist areas it would be advisable to keep holy buildings (which are painted white and have domes/prayer flags and prayer walls *mãné*) to your right.

Lonely Planet also publishes *Trekking in the Indian Himalaya* and *Trekking in the Nepal Himalaya*. Both of these books provide detailed information and route descriptions.

Hiring Porters

Will you come with me?
méré sāth chaléñgé?
I have to go to ....
.... jānā hai
How many days will it take?
kitné din lagéñgé?
What do you charge per day?
ék din kā kyā lété haiñ?

(And) for the horse/mule?
(aur) ghoṛé/khachchar ké liyé?
Including food?
khāné ké sāth?
(And) without food?
(aur) binā (or *bagair*) *khāné ké?*
With a load.
bojh ké sāth
Without a load.
bojh ké binā (or bagair)

Directions

Hill-folk seem to have something against telling trekkers the correct distance to their destination – they normally understate it. Perhaps they don't want to demoralise the trekker by telling the truth. They measure distances in miles, km, *kos* (two to 2½ miles each) or *paṛāo* literally, 'halt' or 'resting point'. A *paṛāo* is equal to what is considered to be the distance that a normal person can trek in one day before resting.

uphill	*charhāī*
downhill	*utār*
far	*dūr*
near	*nazdīk*
this side	*is or*
that side	*us pār*
level	*maidān, barābar* (colloquial)

Along the Way

Unless you are trying out a new route, there will be a place to eat and stay around the time the average trekker feels the need for a meal or rest. As a matter of fact a *paṛāo* is a place to stay (normally a village) more than a measure of distance. If the route is popular enough to justify a government rest house, there will be one. If not, then some local resident will probably have an arrangement with porters to accommodate their clients, for a fee.

Excuse me.
māf kījiyé (literally, 'forgive me')
(Please) listen.
suniyé
Which way is it to ....?
.... *ko kaun sā rāstā hai?*
Where is ....?
.... *kahāñ hai?*
Is there a place to spend the night?
rāt ko rehné kī jagā hai?
What will it cost?
kitnā paisā lagégā?
I will pay.
maiñ paisé dūñgā (m)
maiñ paisé dūñgī (f)
What kind of food is available?
kis qism kā khānā milégā?
How much for the food and shelter?
khāné aur kamré kā kitnā paisā hogā?

Please ask about	.... *ké bāré méñ pūchhīyé*
food	*khāné*
tea	*chāy*
bread	*roṭī*
boiled water	*ublé pānī*

Please give me	*mujhé .... dījīyé*
rice (cooked)	*chāval*
vegetables	*sabzīyāñ*
shelter	*rehné kī jagah*
tea	*chāy*
uncooked rice	*(kachché) chāval*
tobacco	*tambākū*
Is .... available?	*........ miltā hai?*
food	*khānā*
water	*pānī*
Where is the ....?	*........ kahāñ hai?*
village	*gāoñ*
bridge	*pul*
inn	*ḍhābā; hoṭal*
resting place	*rehné kī jagah*
tea house	*chāy kī dukān*
statue	*stechyū*
idol	*mūrti*
Do you have ....?	*āp ké pās .... hai?*
carrying basket	*ṭokrī*
firewood	*īñdhan; jalāné kī lakṛī*
knife	*chhurī; chākū*
bag	*baig; thailā*

A nod, as elsewhere, means 'yes' and shaking of the head means 'no'. However, some people have a particular movement of the head-and-chin which is between a nod and a shake – it would be safe to assume that this means yes.

Yes
jī hāñ, jī, hāñjī (polite) or *hāñ*
No
jī nahīñ (polite); or *nahīñ, nā*

Nature

How far is	.... *kitnī dūr haī*
forest	*jañgal*
hill, mountain	*pahāṛ*
lake	*jhīl*
peak	*choṭī*
pond	*tālāb*
river	*darīyā*
spring	*chashmā*
tree	*péṛ; darakht*
waterfall	*jharnā*

Weather

Today is	*āj* ....
cloudy	*bādal haiñ*
windy	*havādār din hai*
thundery	*bādal garaj rahé haiñ*
stormy	*tūfān ā rahā hai*
rainy	*bārish ho rahī hai*
sunny	*dhūp niklī hai*
foggy	*kohrā chhāya hai*
cold	*ṭhanḍā hai*

Some useful phrases
Will it be cold tomorrow?
kal ṭhanḍā hogā?
Will it be hot tomorrow?
kal garam hogā?
There is a duststorm. (both a question and a statement)
āñdhī chal rahī hai
There is snow.
barf girī hai (both a question and a statement)

Animals

animal(s)	*jānwar*
bear	*bhālū*
camel	*ūñṭ*
cat	*bil-lī*
goat	*bakrī*
lamb	*mémnā*
monkey	*bandar*
mouse/rat	*chuhā*
pig	*sūar*
sheep	*bhéṛ*
spider	*makṛī*
worm	*kīṛā*

Some Useful Phrases

Please come here.
yahāñ āiyégā
Where are you going?
(āp) kahāñ jā rahé haiñ?

Where have you come from?
(āp) kahāñ sé āyé haiñ?
(Are you) Going by yourself?
(āp) akélé jā rahé haiñ?
Where is the toilet?
ṭaṭṭī kahāñ hai?
pākhānā/laṭrīn kahāñ hai?

The polite word for toilet/defecation is *pākhānā* in Urdu and *shauchālyā/shauch* in Hindi. However, your porter in India or Pakistan may not know these words. *Ṭaṭṭī* is understood in Nepal and Bangladesh as well, but isn't the proper word to use with educated people.

(I) have to rest.
ārām karnā hai
Slowly.
āhistā sé
What is the name of the next town/village?
aglé shehar/gāoñ kā kyā nām hai?
Which way is it to ....?
.... *ko kaun sā rastā hai?*
How many days will it take?
kitné din lagéñgé?
How many hours will it take?
kitné ghanṭé lagéñgé?

Some Useful Words

ask	*pūchhnā*
come	*āo, āiyé* (polite)
defecate	*ṭaṭṭī karnā* (crude, but not vulgar)

difficult	*mushkil*
dirty	*gandā*
distance	*dūrī; fāslā*
distant	*dūr*
down	*nīché*
downhill	*utār*
easy	*āsān*
far	*dūr*
fast (speed or dye)	*téz*
go!	*jāo!, jāiyé* (polite)
heavy	*bhārī*
here	*yahāñ*
inn	*ḍhābā; hoṭal*
kerosene	*maṭṭī kā tél; kérosīn*
knife	*chākū*
light (weight)	*halkā*
light (n)	*raushnī*
light (v)	*jalānā*
load (n)	*bhār*
load (v)	*lādnā*
near	*nazdīk*
now	*ab*
OK/all right	*ṭhīk ṭhāk*
pass (mountain)	*gallā* (in Punjab, etc) *lā* (in Buddhist areas: Ladakh, Tibet, etc)
possible	*mumkin*
rock/boulder	*chaṭṭān*
sleep (v)	*sonā*
stone (n)	*patthar*
stove	*chūlhā* (local stove); *sṭov*
temporary (night) shelter	*rain basérā* (H – colloquial)

up	*ūpar*
uphill	*chaṛhāī*
urinate	*péshāb karnā*
walk (v)	*chalnā*
where	*kahāñ*

Food

There is an enormous range of food available in India and Pakistan. Each region has its own culinary specialties but there are also standard dishes, such as (*dāl*, vegetables, rice and *roṭī*), which can be found everywhere. Not all Indian food is 'chilli-hot'; the better restaurants use a variety of spices to flavour the food. Chinese and western food is also widely available.

The vast majority of Hindus have traditionally been vegetarian. Non-vegetarian Hindus tend to avoid eating beef and Muslims don't eat pork.

Meals

khānā (U, mc); *bhojan* (H)

breakfast	*nāshtā*
lunch	*dopehar kā khānā*
dinner	*rāt kā khānā*

Some Useful Phrases

I am feeling thirsty.
pyās lagī hai

I am hungry.
bhūkh lagī hai

I eat rice.
maiñ chāval khātā hūñ (m)
maiñ chāval khātī hūñ (f)

I drink tap water.
maiñ nal ka pānī pītā hūñ (m)
maiñ nal ka pānī pītī hūñ (f)

I smoke cigarettes.
maiñ sigareṭ pītā hūñ (m)
maiñ sigareṭ pītī hūñ (f)

Can I have a little ....?	*mujhé thoṛā sā .... chāhiyé?*
boiled water	*ublā pānī*
more	*aur*
Please give me	*mujhé .... dījiyégā*
cold beer	*ṭhanḍī bīar*
a meal	*khānā*
bread	*roṭī*
I cannot eat	*maiñ .... nahīñ khā saktā* (m) *maiñ .... nahīñ khā saktī* (f)
spicy food	*mirch wālā khānā*
eggs	*anḍā*
I don't eat	*maiñ .... nahīñ khātā* (m) *maiñ .... nahīñ khātī* (f)
any meat	*koī bhī gosht*
fish	*machhlī*

I eat only vegetarian food.
maiñ shākāhārī (or *vaigīṭériyan*) *hūñ*

Indian vegetarians do not eat fish and many don't eat eggs either.

Fruit	*phal*
apple	*séb*
apricot	*khūbānī*
banana	*kélā*
cherry	*chérī*
coconut	*nāriyal*
custard apple	*sharīfā* (mc); *sītāfal*
dates	*khajūr*
grape	*aṅgūr*
guava	*amrūd*
lemon	*nīmbū*
lychee	*līchī*
mango	*ām*
melon	*kharbūjā*
orange	*santarā*
papaya	*papītā*
peach	*āṛū*
pear	*nāshpātī*
plum	*ālubukhārā*
pomegranate	*anār*
sugarcane	*gan-nā*
sultanas	*kishmish*
sweetlime	*mausammī*
tamarind	*imlī*
watermelon	*tarbūjā*

Vegetables	*sabzī ; tarkārī* (curried)
beans – green	*phalī*
– kidney	*rājmā* or *rājmāsh*
cabbage	*gobhī* or *bandgobhī*
cauliflower	*phūlgobhī*
chillies	*mirch*

eggplant	*baiñgan*
garlic	*lehsun*
gourd - bitter	*karélā*
- bottle	*laukī*
ladies' finger	*bhiṇḍī*
lentil/pulse	*dāl*
lettuce	*sāg*
onion	*pyāz*
peas	*maṭar*
potato	*ālū*
pumpkin - round	*péṭhā*
- green, long	*kaddū* (mc)
white radish	*mūlī*
spinach	*pālak*
tomato	*ṭamāṭar*
turnip	*shalgam*

Dairy Food

butter	*makkhan*
cheese (cottage)	*panīr*
clarified butter	*ghī*
curd	*dahī*
whey/buttermilk	*lassī*
cream	*malāī*
milk	*dūdh*

Nuts

almond	*bādām*
cashew	*kājū*
peanuts/groundnuts	*mūngphalī*

Eggs	*anḍā*
boiled	*ublā huā*
scrambled (Indian style)	*bhujiyā*
omlette	*aumléṭ*
Meat	
meat (generic)	*gosht; mīṭ*
mutton	*gosht; mīṭ*
beef	*gāy* (or *bīf*) *kā gosht*
pork	*sūar kā gosht*
chicken	*murg; murgī*
fish	*machhlī*
duck	*battakh*
liver	*kaléjī*
Cereals	
oats	*jau*
rice	*chāval*
wheat	*géhūñ; gandam* (U)
flour	*āṭā*
Beverages	
water	*pānī*
boiled water	*ublā pānī*
hot water	*garam pānī*
cold water	*ṭhanḍā pānī*
ice	*barf*
soda/aerated water	*soḍā*
tea	*chāy*
coffee	*kofī*
without sugar	*binā chīnī ké*
without milk	*binā dūdh ké*

Kashmiri tea	*kehvā* or *kashmīrī kehvā chā*
iced tea	*barf wālī chāy*
(with) plenty of milk	*bahut sé dūdh (ké sāth)*
(make it) real hot	*garmā garam (banāyéñ)*
without salt	*binā namak ké*
beer	*bīar*
alcohol	*sharāb*

Condiments

sauce - local	*chaṭnī*
- western-style	*saus*
vinegar	*sirkā*
salt	*namak*
black pepper	*kalī mirch*
red chilli/chilli powder	*lāl mirch*
green chilli	*harī mirch*
pickle	*achār*
ginger	*adrak*
onion	*pyāz*
garlic	*lehsun*

Eating Out

The richest Indian cuisine is that of Kashmir which has been greatly influenced by the cuisine of Persia and Soviet Central Asia. A proper Kashmiri feast is considered incomplete without more than 100 different meat dishes.

At five-star hotels you can splash out on a wonderful buffet meal (often serving *tandūrī*, Indian, Chinese and western dishes) and at the other end of the scale you can eat a *thālī* or even more simple than that - *dāl bhāt* - rice and lentils.

If you have over-dosed on chilli don't reach out for a drink; try eating some curd (yoghurt) and/or fruit.

Some Useful Phrases

(A table) for four.
chār logoñ ké liyé (ṭébal)
What do you have?
kyā kyā hai?
Have you eaten?
āpné khā liyā?
I've eaten already.
maiñné khā liyā
Can we order some food?
(kyā ham khānā) orḍar kar sakté haiñ?
We/I would like some food.
khānā chāhiyé
Do you have drinking water?
pīné kā pānī hai?
I like hot and spicy food.
mujhé garam, masālédār khānā pasand hai
I don't like spices and chillies.
mujhé mirch masālā pasand nahīñ
What do you have that's special?
khās kyā hai?
What does this have in it?
is méñ kyā kyā hai?
We'll have one bottle of beer.
ham ék botal bīar léñgé
(Enough) for four people.
chār logoñ ké liyé
I didn't order this.
maiñné yé nahīñ māñgā thā

Some Useful Words

fork	*kāñṭā*
spoon	*chammach*
knife	*chhurī*
plate	*pléṭ; thālī* (steel)
straw (drinking)	*pāip; strau*
curry	*tarkārī; karī*
dry/without gravy	*sūkhā/binā tari ké*
without curry or spices	*binā mirch masālé ké*
boiled	*ublā huā*
without chillies	*binā mirch ké*
without spices	*binā masālé ké*
permitted to Muslims	*halāl*
forbidden to Muslims	*harām*

To eat a *thālī* is generally an inexpensive fixed-menu (rice, *dāl*, vegetable curry, *roṭī* and curd), fixed-price meal.

North Indian/Pakistani Food

Within the subcontinent this food is known as 'Mughlai' - *muglāī* - the food of the Mughals.

Bread

roṭī - bread
tandūrī roṭī - baked in the earthen Indian oven (the *tandūr*); is thick and has many layers
nān - spade shaped; very thick and soft
parāñṭhā or *paroṭhā* - fried *roṭī*; sometimes stuffed (vegetable *parāñṭhā*, egg *parāñṭhā* and in Tamil Nadu, the exquisite Ceylon *parāñṭhā*, which is a meal in itself, with meat and other stuffing)
bréḍ, ḍabbal roṭī - western-style bread

Fried bread
pūrī - deep fried
bhaṭūra - thick large puri
shīrmāl - sweet, very heavy, fried bread

Rice
chāval - rice; boiled or steamed
pulāo - north Indian fried rice; normally vegetarian
biryānī - Hyderabad-style rice, normally combined with mutton or chicken; flavoured with spices

Non-vegetarian dishes
kormā - curry; mutton, chicken, fish, etc
rogan josh - minced meat
koftā - ball of minced meat; (or vegetables - in which case they will specify vegetable *koftā*)
kabāb - minced meat moulded into one of two common shapes:
sīkh kabāb - hollow, cylindrical kabab; eaten mostly during the day; cooked on skewers
shāmī kabāb - like a thick coin; 'the evening kabab'
tandūri chicken - whole chicken, smeared with spices, baked in the Indian earthen oven (the *tandūr*); without gravy

Vegetarian dishes
maṭar - peas; normally curried
panīr - cottage cheese; curried or fried
maṭar panīr - peas and cheese curry
bhinḍī - ladies' finger (okra); usually uncurried
phalī - green beans; sometimes eaten in the pod
bhurtā (or *bhartā*) - mashed eggplant

dāl - lentils
Normally vegetables are curried. Other vegetables are listed in the Vegetable section on page 54.

Lentils

chanā - the standard lentils; curried or heavily spiced; the latter type is a favourite road-side snack in the Hindi/Urdu areas and is eaten with a fried slice of bread; this combination is called *chanā bhaṭūrā*
chholā bhaṭūrā - flavoured with lemon juice, onions and other brackish spices
rongī - small, mustard-coloured beans; the kind used in baked beans; curried or served with thick paste
rājmā - kidney beans; curried or with thick paste
arhar - large, yellowish-brown pulse; normally curried
māsh/urad (polished) - yellowish-white, biggish grained pulse; normally served in a viscous form
urad (unpolished) - black gram
mūn̄g - yellowish-green gram
masūr - pulse that is red when uncooked; yellowish-red when cooked

South Indian Food

Inexpensive throughout India, it has become the favourite snack food of India and parts of Sri Lanka. South Indian food in this context is really the cuisine of Tamil Nadu, Karnataka and parts of Andhra Pradesh. Liberal amounts of *chaṭnī* (mostly coconut) spice the meal.

rasam - a lentil based curry, often with all kinds of vegetables added
dosā - a large pancake made from rice flour; fried brown and

crisp; eaten with chutney and *rasam*

masālā dosā - potatoes (sometimes other vegetables) stuffed into a *dosā*

vaṛā or *vadā* - thick ring made of mashed pulses; brownish-yellow outside and white under the crust; served with chutney and *rasam*

idlī - cakes of rice; bland, steamed and served with *rasam* and chutney

chaṭnī - normally coconut based

Kashmiri Food

Boiled rice serves as the base. There are too many Kashmiri dishes to name, but here are a few of them.

goshtābā - huge meat ball cooked in curds; the meat in this dish is not minced with metal knives but pounded with wooden pounders

rishtā - smaller meat ball; curried, instead of being cooked in curds/milk

yakhnī - meat cooked in milk/curds

tabak māz - grilled ribs

martsvāngan kormā - mutton curry, reddened with a local chilli; normally very spicy

rogan josh - mutton curry, with plenty of ghee

panīr yakhnī - cottage cheese cooked in milk/curds, normally along with the large leafed local lettuce, *hak sāg*

Sweets

The Bengalis are regarded as the sweet experts of the subcontinent. The Kashmiris and Ladakhis, who live miles away from the sugarcane growing areas, have no traditional sweets at all though the Kashmiris are wizards with baked sweet dishes.

khoyā - milk in a solidified form, the result of much condensation and drying; the base of most milk-based South Asian sweets but not a sweet by itself
ras gullā - literally means 'the ball of juice'; white; normally served chilled in syrup
gulāb jāmun - brown ball, white inside; fried and served hot in a rose-water syrup
khīr - the Indian 'custard'; a thick, white 'custard' made of milk and rice; served hot or chilled; Muslims eat it to break the Ramadan fast
barfī - the standard sweet; a solid, sweetened *khoya*; served in small slices; has many variations such as chocolate, coconut, almond, etc
laḍḍū - yellow balls, lentil-based
gājar kā halwā - made from carrot, milk and sweet spices
kaṛā - a cereals and ghee-based paste; the Sikh prayer offering
rasmalāī - literally means 'cream and juice'; a mixture of thickened cream, milk and syrup; served chilled
rabṛī - sweet, coagulated, granular milk
kulfī - the Mughal ice cream; pistachio flavoured

baker selling nan (bread)

Shopping

Unless you are purchasing handicrafts from a government-run shop, you can be confident that bargaining will help bring the price down considerably, maybe by half. Consumer goods, manufactured for distribution through a large number of retail outlets, normally have the price printed on them. This price is rarely negotiable.

While pavement shops bring down prices considerably on bargaining, even the plushest of shops will often give discounts.

Every city in the subcontinent has a congested market, where goods are sold at prices considerably lower than in the shops. The market area is generally an atmospheric and intriguing area to wander around.

Where is the ....?	.... *kahāñ hai?*
shop	*dukān*
market	*bāzār; maṛkiṭ*
barber	*nāī* (H & U); *hajjām* (U)
chemist	*davāī kī dukān*
book shop	*kitāb kī dukān*
cobbler	*mochī*
shoeshop	*jūtoñ kī dukān*
cloth/clothes shop	*kapṛoñ kī dukān*
tailor	*darzī*
teastall	*chāy kī dukān*

How much? (does it cost)
kitnā?

(I) don't want (it).
nahīñ chāhiyé
It costs too much.
bahut zyādā hai

How much will .... cost?	.... *kī kyā kīmat hai?*
this	*is*
fruit	*phal*
this fruit	*is phal*
one kg	*ék kilo*
one metre	*ék mīṭar*
one (piece)	*ék*
both	*dono*

How much will three (of these) cost (if bought together).
tīn léñ to kyā kīmat hogī?

Do you have .... ?	*āp ké pās .... hai?*
newspaper(s)	*akhbār*
matches	*māchis*
mosquito repellent	*machchhar mārné wālī davā*
paper	*kāgaz*
envelope	*lifāfā*
shoulder bag	*jholā*
soap	*sābun*
map	*nakshā*

Where can I buy	.... *kahāñ kharīd sakté haiñ?*
string	*dhāgā*
film	*film*

I want	*mujhé........ chāhiyé*
a book	*kitāb*
cigarettes	*sigareṭ*
shoes	*jūté*
socks	*jurāb, mozé*
shirt	*kamīz*

I am looking for	*ham .... ḍhūñḍh rahé haiñ*
cooking pot	*patīlā*
jewellery	*gehné, zévar*

Some Useful Words

cotton thread	*sūt*
cotton (adj)	*sūtī*
cotton material	*sūtī kapṛā*
silk	*résham* (n); *réshamī* (adj, silken)
wool	*ūn* (n); *ūnī* (adj, woollen)
bottle	*botal*
mirror	*shīshā*
glass (or metal!) tumbler	*gilās*
pen	*kalam*

Other goods, such as pencils, toilet paper, toothpaste, brush – *burush*!, etc, as in English. Sanitary napkins and mosquito repellent are known better by their brand names.

Bargaining

I don't have much money.
méré pās zyādā/bahut paisé nahīñ haiñ
That's too much.
bahut zyādā hai

(I will) give .... rupees.
  .... *rupayé dūñgā* (m)
  .... *rupayé dūñgī* (f)
How many rupees?
  kitné rupayé?
Can you bring the price down?
  kīmat (or *dām*) *kam kar sakté haiñ?*
The price is too much.
  kīmat bahut zyādā hai
(I) won't give more than ....
  .... *sé zyādā nahīñ dūñgā* (m)
  .... *sé zyādā nahīñ dūñgī* (f)
Do you have something cheaper?
  is sé sastā kuchh hai?
If (I) buy two .... will the price come down?
  do .... léñ to kīmat kam hogī?
The quality is not good.
  māl achchhā nahīñ hai
What's your lowest price?
  āp kī sab sé kam kīmat kyā hai?

this one	*yé wālā*
that one	*vo wālā*
which one?	*kaun sā?*
too big	*bahut baṛā*
too small	*bahut chhoṭā*
too long	*bahut lambā*
too short	*bahut chhoṭā*
too tight	*bahut tañg*
too loose/wide	*bahut ḍhīlā/chauṛā*
not enough	*kāfī nahīñ*; or *kam hai* (too little)

still not enough	*ab bhī kam hai*
good enough	*ṭhīk hai*
expensive	*meheñgā* or *maingā*
cheap	*sastā*
too expensive	*bahut meheñgā*

Can I see that?
kyā maiñ vo dékh saktā hūñ? (m)
kyā maiñ vo dékh saktī hūñ? (f)
Please show another kind/style.
koi aur qism/sṭāil dikhāiyé
Do you have (any) more?
āp ké pās (kuchh) aur haiñ?
The sleeves are too long.
bāzū bahut lambé haiñ
(Do you have) anything larger than this?
is sé baṛā hai?
How much for both?
dono kā kitnā?
How much all together?
kul milā kar kitnā?
good quality (stuff)
baṛhīyā (māl)

Colours	*rang*
white	*suféd*
green	*harā* (m); *harī* (f)
pink	*gulābi*
black	*kālā* (m); *kālī* (f)
red	*lāl*
grey	*saléṭī*
brown	*bhūrā*

blue	*nīlā*
purple	*baiñganī*
yellow	*pīlā*
dark–	*gehrā*
light–	*halkā*

Gems & Jewellery

ring	*añgūṭhī*
necklace	*hār*
bead, flower-garland	*mālā*
bracelet – for women	*kañgan*
– for men (especially Sikhs)	*kaṛā*
gem(s)	*javāhar -(āt)*
jewellery	*zévar, gehné*
ruby	*lāl*
diamond	*hīrā*
gold	*sonā*
silver	*chāñdī*
bronze	*tāmbā*
sapphire	*nīlam*
brass	*pītal*
emerald	*pannā*
pearl	*motī*

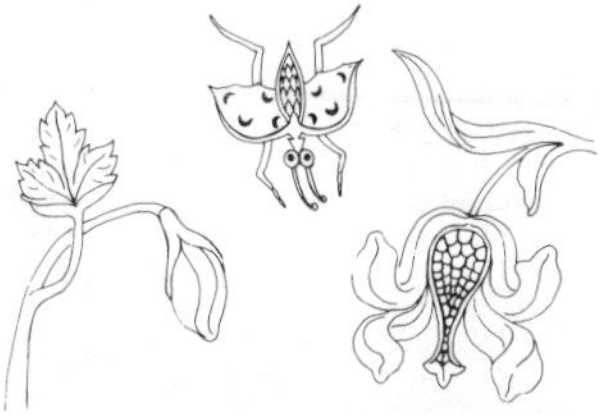

Health

There are a few medical alternatives open to those who are unfortunate enough to become ill. Firstly there are doctors trained in western medicine. They practise from the mission hospitals, government hospitals and private practice. There are also practitioners of the traditional Indian *ayurvedic* system of medicine and the Greco-Islamic *unani* system. Doctors trained in western medicine have had all their education in English.

Where is the ....?	*........ kahāñ hai?*
doctor	*ḍokṭar*
– ayurvedic	*vaid; vaidya*
– unani	*hakīm*
dentist	*dāntoñ kā ḍokṭar*
hospital	*haspatāl*
chemist's shop	*davāī kī dukān*
........'s house	*........ kā ghar*

I have a	*mujhé .... hai*
cold	*zukām*
fever	*bukhār*
dysentery	*péchish ho gayī*

My .... aches/hurts.	*........ méñ dard hai*
stomach	*méré péṭ*
chest	*mérī chhātī*
back	*mérī pīṭh*

My stomach is upset.
mérā péṭ kharāb hai
I have a sore throat.
mérā galā kharāb hai
It hurts here.
yahāñ dard hai
I can't sleep.
maiñ so nahīñ saktā (m)
maiñ so nahīñ saktī (f)
I have been like this for (two) weeks.
maiñ is hāl méñ (do) haftoñ sé hūñ
Is it serious?
kyā yé sīrias/khatarnāk hai?

Parts of the Body

arm	*bāzū; bāñh*
back	*pīṭh*
breasts	*chhātiyāñ; stan* (H)
chest	*sīnā*
ears	*kān*
eyes	*āñkh*
finger(s)	*uñglī(-yāñ)*
hand(s)	*hāth*
head	*sir; sar*
leg(s)	*ṭāñg (-géñ)*
liver	*kaléjā; kaléjī*
lungs	*phéphaṛé*
mouth	*muh; muñh*
nose	*nāk*
shoulder	*kandhā*
throat	*galā*
tongue	*jībh; zubān*

Complaints

anaemia	*khūn kī kamī*
cholera	*haizā*
constipation	*kabz*
cough	*khāñsī*
cramps	*maroṛ; nas chaṛhnā*
diabetes	*daībitīs*
diarrhoea	*péchish*
dysentery	*péchish; julāb* (mc)
headache	*sar dard*
impotence	*nāmardgī; khoī huī tāqat*
influenza	*flū; miyādī bukhār*
malaria	*malériyā*
pneumonia	*nimoniā*
rabies	*kutté kī bīmārī; rébīz*
sprain	*moch*
stomachache	*péṭ dard*
toothache	*dāñt dard*
venereal disease	*gupt rog; kām rog* (H); *jinsī bīmārī* (U)

Medication — *davāī*

pill	*golī*
sleeping pill	*nīñd kī golī*
plaster	*palastar*

How much (money) per tablet?
ék golī kī kyā kīmat?
How many times a day?
din méñ kitnī bār?
(four) times a day
din méñ (chār) bār

I'm allergic to penicillin.
mujhé pénicilin sé élargī hai

Aspirin, injection, operation, band aid, etc, as in English or by their brand name.

Some Useful Phrases

I am tired.
maiñ thakā huā hūñ (m)
maiñ thakī huī hūñ (f)
I need a doctor.
mujhé ḍokṭar chāhiyé
I have (vomited) several times.
mujhé kaī bār (ulṭī/kai) huī hai

Some Useful Words

accident	*aiksiḍenṭ; ṭakkar* (collision)
addict	*ādī*
addiction	*lat*
address	*patā*
allergy	*élargī*
bandage	*paṭṭī*
beware	*hoshiyār*
bleed	*khūn behnā*
blood	*khūn*
bone	*haḍḍī*
faint	*béhosh*
insane	*pāgal*
itch	*khujlī*
lice	*jūéñ*
nurse (n)	*nars*
pain	*dard*

patient (n)	*marīz*
pharmacy	*davāī kī dukān*
poison	*zehar*
pregnant	*hāmilā* (U); *garbhvatī* (H)
prescription	*priskripshan; nuskhā*
skin	*chamṛī* (mc); *tvachā* (H)
vitamin	*viṭāmin*

Time & Dates

The traditional Indian system of telling the time is the *pehar* system where the days are divided into *pehars*. Nowadays the western system of telling time is used and understood all over the subcontinent.

What time is it?
kyā ṭāim huā?
What hour is it?
kitné bajé haiñ?
How long (will it/you take)?
kitnī dér hai?
Will it/you take time?
dér lagégī?

In popular parlance there are no local equivalents for am or pm, the hour is referred to as such and such hour of the day or night. For example:

the hour	**referred to as**	**literally**
12 noon	*dopehar ké bārah bajé*	12 in the afternoon
12 midnight	*rāt ké bārah bajé*	12 at night
5 am	*subah ké pāñch bajé*	5 in the morning
5 pm	*shām ké pāñch bajé*	5 in the evening
4 am	*subah* (or *rāt*)	4 in the morning/night
4 pm	*dopehar ké chār bajé* (or *shām) ké chār bajé*)	4 in the afternoon/evening

morning	*subah*
afternoon	*dopehar*
evening	*shām*
night	*rāt*
midnight	*ādhī rāt*
9 o'clock	*nau bajé*

In the subcontinent 5 am is generally considered to be the start of the day.

The *Shak* calendar has been adopted by the Government of India as the national calendar, along with the Gregorian calendar. Both are solar calendars; *Chaitra 1* falls on 22 March normally and on 21 March in a leap year. It is 78 years behind the Gregorian calendar. Thus 1988 AD is 1909-1910 of the *Shak* era.

The *Hijri* calendar has been adopted by the Governments of Pakistan and Bangladesh as the official calendar. It is a lunar calendar and 1980 AD corresponded to 1400 After Hijri.

Months

January	*janvarī*
February	*farvarī*
March	*mārch*
April	*aprail*
May	*maī*
June	*jūn*
July	*julāī*
August	*agast*
September	*sitambar*
October	*aktūbar*
November	*navambar*
December	*disambar*

Days

Monday	*somvār* (H & U)	*pīr* (U)
Tuesday	*mañgalvār*	
Wednesday	*budhvār*	
Thursday	*brihaspativār* (H)	*jumérāt* (U)
Friday	*shukrvār* (H)	*jumā* (U)
Saturday	*shanīvār*	
Sunday	*ravīvār* (H)	*itvār* (U)

Present Time

today	*āj*
this evening	*āj shām*
tonight	*āj rāt*
in this month	*is mahīné*
all day long	*sārā din*

Past Time

The words for yesterday/tomorrow, the day before/the day after are the same. Therefore clarifying phrases have been included.

yesterday	*kal* (or *bītā huā kal* – the day that has gone)
day before yesterday	*parsoñ* (or *bītā huā parsoñ*)
last week	*pichhlé hafté*
two weeks ago	*do hafté pehlé*
three months ago	*tīn mahīné pehlé*
four years ago	*chār sāl pehlé*

Future Time

tomorrow	*kal* (or *āné wālā kal* – the day still to come)

day after tomorrow	*parsoñ* (or *āné wālā parsoñ*)
next week	*aglé hafté*
next month	*aglé mahīné*
two more months	*do mahīné aur*
three months later	*tīn mahīné bād*

Some Useful Phrases

I will stay here for two months.
maiñ yahāñ do mahīné rahūñgā (m)
maiñ yahāñ do mahīné rahūñgī (f)

What month is this?
yé kaun sā mahīnā hai?

What is the date today?
āj kyā tārīkh hai?

How long have you been here?
āp yahāñ kab sé haiñ?

I'm going to Hyderabad for three weeks.
maiñ tīn hafté ké liyé haidrābād jā rahā hūñ (m)
maiñ tīn hafté ké liyé haidrābād jā rahī hūñ (f)

Any time at all.
kabhī bhī

Some Useful Words

annual	*sālānā*
before	*pehlé*
century	*sadī* (U, mc); *shatābadī* (H)
date	*tārīkh*
dawn	*subah; prātah* (H)
day	*din*
daytime	*din kā vakt*
decade	*dashak* (H)
early	*jaldī*

evening	*shām*
everyday	*rozānā*
forever	*haméshā ké liyé*
fortnight	*paksh* (H)
holiday	*chhuṭṭī*
late	*dér*
now	*ab*
nowadays	*ājkal*
period (era)	*daur* (U, mc); *kāl* (H)
time	*vakt*
on time	*vakt par*
in time	*vakt méñ*
until	*jab tak*
when	*kab*
whenever	*jab bhī*
minute(s)	*minaṭ*
hour	*ghanṭā*
hours	*ghanṭé*
a month and a half	*ḍéṛh mahīnā*
year	*sāl*
sometimes	*kabhī kabhī*

Numbers

Hindi

1	१	2	२	3	३	4	४	5	५
6	६	7	७	8	८	9	९	10	१०

Urdu

1	۱	2	۲	3	۳	4	۴	5	۵
6	۶	7	۷	8	۸	9	۹	10	۱۰

1	*ék*
2	*do*
3	*tīn*
4	*chār*
5	*pāñch*
6	*chha*
7	*sāt*
8	*āṭh*
9	*nau*
10	*das*
11	*gyārah*
12	*bārah*
13	*térah*
14	*chaudah*
15	*pandrah*

16	*solah*
17	*satrah; sattārah*
18	*aṭhṭhārah*
19	*unnīs*
20	*bīs*
21	*ikkīs*
22	*bāis*
23	*téis*
24	*chaubīs*
25	*pachchīs*
26	*chhabbīs*
27	*sattāīs*
28	*aṭhṭhāis*
29	*unnattīs*
30	*tīs*
31	*ikkattīs*
32	*battīs*
33	*tétīs; taiñtīs*
34	*chauñtīs*
35	*paiñtīs*
36	*chhattīs*
37	*saiñtīs*
38	*aṛatīs*
39	*untālīs*
40	*chālīs*
41	*iktālīs*
42	*bayālīs*
43	*taiñtālīs*
44	*chauvālīs*
45	*paiñtālīs*
46	*chhiyālīs*
47	*saiñtālīs*

48	*arṭālīs*
49	*unanchās; unchās*
50	*pachās*
51	*ikkyāvan*
52	*bāvan*
53	*trépan*
54	*chauvan*
55	*pachpan*
56	*chhappan*
57	*sattāvan*
58	*aṭhāvan*
59	*unsaṭh*
60	*sāṭh*
61	*iksaṭh*
62	*bāsaṭh*
63	*trésaṭh*
64	*chauñsaṭh*
65	*paiñsaṭh*
66	*chhiyāsaṭh*
67	*saṛsaṭh*
68	*aṛsaṭh*
69	*unhattar*
70	*sattar*
71	*ikhattar*
72	*bahattar*
73	*téhattar*
74	*chauhattar*
75	*pachhattar*
76	*chhihattar*
77	*sathattar*
78	*aṭhhattar*
79	*unāsī*

80	*assī*
81	*ikāsī*
82	*bayāsī*
83	*térāsī*
84	*chaurāsī*
85	*pachāsī*
86	*chhiyāsī*
87	*satāsī*
88	*aṭhāsī*
89	*navāsī*
90	*nabbé; navvé*
91	*ikānavé*
92	*bānavé*
93	*térānavé*
94	*chaurānavé*
95	*pachānavé*
96	*chhiyānavé*
97	*sattānavé*
98	*aṭhānavé*
99	*ninnānavé*
100	*ék sau*
200	*do sau*
300	*tīn sau*; and so on
339	*tīn sau untālīs*
1000	*ék hazār*
7809	*sāt hazār āth sau nau*
10,000	*das hazār*
13,002	*térah hazār do*
1,00,000	*lākh; ék lākh* (one lakh)
1,00,00,000	*karoṛ; ék karoṛ* (one crore)
1,00,00,00,000	*arab*
1,00,00,00,00,000	*kharab*

No pattern emerges from one to 100, but after that the sequence is the same as in English. For example: 9249 – nine thousand two hundred (and) forty-nine becomes *nau hazār do sau unchās*. In the subcontinent, the way numbers are divided up by the use of commas is different to the method commonly employed in the west.

Even though most South Asian countries have officially adopted the metric system, when dealing with sums of money the practice (in Government as well as business circles) is to talk of lakhs and crores of rupees but millions of foreign currency (dollars, roubles, yen, etc).

Ordinal Numbers

first	*pehlā*
second	*dūsrā*
third	*tīsrā*
fourth	*chauthā*
fifth	*pāñchvāñ*
sixth	*chhaṭhā*
seventh	*sātvāñ*

(eighth onwards: suffix *-vāñ* to the number concerned)

Fractions

one-quarter	*chauthā* (fourth); *ék chauthāī* (one fourth)
one-half	*ādhā*
three-quarters	*paunā* (a quarter short) or *pauné ék*
(the) whole	*pūrā*
one and a quarter	*savā*; (or *savā ék*)
one and a half	*ḍéṛh*
one and three-quarters	*pauné do*

two and a quarter	*savā do* (and so on for 3¼)
two and a half	*ḍhāī; aṛhāī* (U)
two and three-quarters	*pauné tīn* (and so on for 3¾)

3½, 4½, etc, follow a regular pattern *sāṛhé tīn; sāṛhé chār*

Some Useful Words

count (v)	*gino, giniyé* (polite)
count(-ing) (n)	*gintī*
dozen	*darjan; darzan*
equal	*barābar*
half	*ādhā*
little (amount)	*thoṛā*
many	*bahut*
maximum	*zyādā sé zyādā*
minimum	*kam sé kam*
pair	*joṛā*
size (tailoring)	*nāp; māp*
weight	*vazan*

Vocabulary

A

about (some one) - *bāré mén*
about (near) - *ās pās*
ache (n & v) - *dard*
addict (n) - *ādī*
address - *patā*
adult - *bālig* (U), *vayask* (H)
advertisement - *ishtéhār*
aeroplane - *havāī jahāz*
after - *-ké bād*
agriculture - *khétī bāṛi* (colloquial)
age - *umr*
all - *sab*
alone - *akélā*
alcohol - *sharāb*
always - *haméshā*
among- - *-méṅ*
ancient - *purānā*
animal - *jānvar*
ant - *chyūṅṭī; chīṅṭī*
anywhere - *kahīṅ bhī*
application - *arzī*
argument - *behas*
around - *ās pās*
arrangement - *silsilā*
artist - *kalākār* (H); *fankār* (U)
assistance - *madad*
attorney - *vakīl*

B

bad – *kharāb; burā*
bangle – *chūṛī*
barber – *nāī* (H & U); *hajjām* (U)
bargaining – *saudé bāzī*
bathe (v) – *nahānā*
because – *kyoñki*
bed – *bistar*
bee (honey-) – *shehad kī makkhī*
before – *pehlé*
beggar – *bhīkārī*
behind – *pīchhé*
betel (leaf) – *pān*
between – *bīch méñ*
big – *baṛā*
bill – *bil*
bill (money) – *noṭ*
bird – *chiṛīyā*
birthday – *sālgirā* (U); *janm din* (H)
bleed – *khūn behnā*
blood – *khūn*
blow (at) – *phūk mārnā*
blow (of wind) – *havā chalnā*
blue – *nīlā*
board (to climb) (v) – *chaṛhnā*
board (wooden) – *phaṭṭā*
boat – *kishtī*
boil (v) – *ubālnā*
boiled – *ublā huā*
bone – *haḍḍī*
book – *kitāb*
bookshop – *kitāb kī dukān*

border (of garment) - *kinārā*
border (of nation) - *sīmā* (H); *sarhad* (U)
borrow (v) - *udhār lénā*
both - *dono*
bottle (n) - *botal*
boy - *laṛkā*
bracelet (female) - *kangan*
bracelet (male) - *kaṛā*
brave - *bahādur*
bread - *roṭī*
break (v) - *toṛnā*
breakfast - *nāshtā*
breath - *sāṅs*
bring! - *lāo!*
bring (v) - *lānā*
broken - *ṭūṭā huā*
broom - *jhāṛū*
brother - *bhāī*
brown - *bhūrā*
bus - *bas*
business - *kārobār*
businessman (trader etc) - *saudāgar*
buy (v) - *kharīdnā*

C

calm - *shānt* (H); *pur aman* (U)
cancel (v) - *radd karnā*
candle - *mom battī*
capable - *qābil*
car - *kār; gāṛī*
careful! - *hoshiyār!*
careful (adj) - *satark* (H); *ehtiyāt mand* (U)

cat - *bil-lī*
cave - *gufā*
chair - *kursī*
charity - *khairāt* (H & U); *dān* (H)
cheap (inexpensive) - *sastā*
chess - *shatranj*
chew - *chabānā*
chicken - *murgī*
child - *bachchā*
children - *bachché*
chilli - *mirch (ī)*
chin - *ṭhuḍḍī*
chocolate - *chaukléṭ*
cholera - *haizā*
choose (v) - *pasand karnā*
cinema - *pikchar; sanīmā*
circle - *dāyarā* (H & U); *chakr* (H)
citizen - *nāgarik*
clean (adj) - *sāf*
climb (n) - *chaṛhāī*
climb (v) - *chaṛhnā*
close (adj) (near) - *nazdīk*
close (v) (to shut) - *band karnā*
clothing - *kapṛé*
cloud - *bādal*
coconut - *nāriyal*
coffee - *kofī; kāpī* (south Indian)
coins - *sikké*
cold (temperature) - *ṭhanḍā*
cold (ailment) - *zukām*
colour (n) - *rang*
comb (n) - *kanghī*

comfortable (eg, chair) - *ārāmdéh*
comfortable (are you?) - *ārām sé (haiñ?)*
commerce - *vyāpār; byopār*
company (friends) - *sāthī*
complaint - *shikāyat*
confirmation - *tas dīq* (U); *pakkā karnā*
constipation - *kabz*
conversation - *bāt chīt*
cook (v) - *pakānā*
cook (n) - *khānsāmā*
copy (to imitate) - *nakal karnā*
corner - *konā*
cough - *khāñsī*
cow - *gāy*
crack - *darār*
crazy - *dīwānā; pāgal*
crooked (man or thing) - *ṭéṛhā*
crossroad - *chaurāhā; chaurastā*
crowd - *bhīṛ*
crowded - *bharā huā*
cup - *kap; pyālī*
curious - *ajīb; vichitra*
cushion (n) - *gaddā*

D

damp - *gīlā*
date - *tārīkh*
day - *din*
day after tomorrow - *āné wālā parsoñ*
daylight - *din kī roshnī*
death - *maut*
delicious - *mazédār; swādisht*

dentist - *dāñtoñ kā ḍokṭar*
depart (v) - *jānā*
descend - *utarnā*
destination - *manzil*
destruction - *tabāhī*
diarrhoea - *patlā dast*
die (v) - *marnā*
different - *bhinna* (H); *farak* (U)
difficult - *mushkil*
dinner - *rāt kā khānā*
diplomat - *safīr* (U); *rājdūt*
dirty - *gandā*
discover (v) - *ḍhūñḍh nikālnā*
disease - *bīmārī*
dissolve (v) - *ghulnā*
dive (v) - *ḍubkī lagānā*
divorce - *talāq*
doctor - *ḍokṭar*
document - *kāgaz*
dog - *kuttā*
door - *darvāzā*
dress (v) - *kapṛé pehannā*
dress (n) - *kapṛā*
drink (v) - *pīnā*
drink (n) - *pīné kī chīz*
drug - *davā*
drug store - *davāī kī dukān*
drum (musical) - *ḍhol*
drum (container) - *(baṛā) pīpā*
dry (adj) - *sukhā*
dry (v) - *sūkhānā*
during - *-ké darmiyān*

dust - *dhūl*
dysentery - *péchish; julāb*

E

each - *har ék*
early - *jaldī*
east - *pūrab*
eat (v) - *khānā*
eat! - *khāo*; *khāiyé* (polite)
edge (n) - *konā; dhār* (in blade, etc)
egg - *anḍā*
electricity - *bijlī*
empty (adj & v) - *khālī*
end - *khatam*
endorsement - *inḍorsmént; tāīd* (U)
enough - *kāfī*
envelope (n) - *lifāfā*
event - *vāqiyā* (U); *ghaṭnā* (H)
every - *har*
exact - *bilkul ṭhīk*
examine - *gaur karnā*
expensive - *mehañgā*
expert - *māhir* (U); *vishéshagya* (H)
extinguish - *bujhānā*
extra - *zyādā* (U); *atirikt* (H)
extremely - *bahut*

F

factory - *kārkhānā; faikṭarī*
faith (confidence) - *aitbār*
faith (religious, etc) - *yaqīn* (mc); *shraddhā* (H)
fake - *jālī*

farmer - *kisān*
fast (speedy) (ad) - *téz*
fast (no food) - *rozā* (M); *vrat* (H)
father - *vālid* (U); *pitā* (H)
fever - *bukhār*
few (little/short) - *kam*
few - *kuchh*
film - *film; rīl*
fine (good) - *achchhā*
fine (penalty) - *jurmānā*
finish (v) - *khatm karnā*
fire (n) - *āg*
first - *pehlā*
fish (n) - *machchhī; machalī*
flavour - *zāyaqā* (U); *svād* (H)
float (v) - *tairnā*
flour - *āṭā*
flower (n) - *phūl*
follow, chase - *pīchhā karnā*
foreign - *vidéshī* (mc); *bairūnī* (U)
foreigner - *pardésī*
forest - *jañgal*
fork - *kāñṭā*
fortune - *kismat*
fortune teller - *jyotishī* (H)
fountain - *jharnā*
fragrant - *khushbūdār*
French - *frānsīsī*
fresh - *tāzā*
friend - *dost*
friendly - *dostānā*
frog - *méñḍhak*

fry (v) - *talnā*
full - *bharā huā*
fun - *mazā*
funeral - *kriyā karam* (H); *tadfīn* (U)

G

garden - *bāg*
gather (v) - *ikaṭṭhā karnā*
genuine - *asal; aslī*
girl - *laṛkī*
give (v) - *dénā*
give & take - *lén-dén*
glass (mirror) - *shīshā*
glass (tumbler) - *gilās* (even if made of metal!)
glue - *gond̐* (gum)
go (v) - *jānā*
go! - *jāo!; jāiyé* (polite)
gold - *sonā*
gong - *ghanṭā*
green - *harā*
grill, roast (v) - *bhūnnā*
guest - *mehmān*
guide - *gāiḍ; rāstā dikhāné wālā*

H

half - *ādhā*
hammer - *hathauṛā*
hand-made - *hāth sé banā*
harbour (n) - *bandargāh*
hat/cap - *ṭopī*
head - *sir; sar*
headache - *sar dard*

health - *séhat*
help (n) - *madad*
help (v) - *madad karnā*
help! - *bachāo!*; *madad kījiyé* (please assist me)
hill - *pahāṛ*
hire (v) - *kirāyé lénā*
holiday - *chhuṭṭī*
hollow - *khokhlā*
honest - *īmāndār*
horn (animals) - *sīṅg*
horse - *ghoṛā*
hospital - *aspatāl*
hot - *garam*
hotel - *hoṭal*
hour - *ghanṭā*
hunt (n) - *shikār*
hurt (n) - *choṭ*
husband - *khāvind* (U); *patī* (H)

I

identification - *pehchān* (colloquial)
immediate - *fauran*
indigenous - *désī* (colloquial)
industry - *sannat* (U); *udyog* (H)
infection - *chūt, sankramana*
insane - *pāgal*
insect - *kīṛā*
inside - *andar*
insurance - *bīmā* (H)
interesting - *dilchasp*
intersection - *chaurāhā*
iron - *lohā*

island – *jazīrā* (U); *dwīp* (H)
itch – *khārish; khujlī*
ivory – *hāthī dāṅt*

J

jar (glazed; for pickles etc) – *martabān*
jewel – *nagīnā*
jewellery – *zévar* (sing); *zévarāt* (pl)
juice (as in fruit) – *ras*
orange juice – *santaré kā ras*

K

kerosene – *miṭṭī kā tél; kéṛosin*
kill (v) – *mārnā*
kilometre – *kilomīṭar*
knife – *chākū; chhurī*

L

lake – *jhīl*
language – *zubān* (U & mc); *bhāshā* (H)
late – *dér*
launderer – *dhobī*
laundry (clothes for) – *dhoné ké kapṛé*
learn (v) – *sīkhnā*
leather – *chamṛā*
leech – *joṅk*
left (hand) – *bāyéṅ*
leg – *ṭāṅg*
letter (mail) – *chiṭṭhī*
letter (of alphabet) – *akshar* (H); *harf* (U)
lice – *jūéṅ* (pl); *jūṅ* (sing)
lightning – *bijlī*

like (v & n) - *pasand*
listen (v) - *sunnā*
listen! - *suno; suniyé* (polite)
live (v) - *jīnā*
live (adj, alive) - *zindā*
loose - *ḍhīlā*
lose (v - an object) - *khonā; gum jānā;*
lose (v - a game) - *hārnā*
lost - *khoyā huā; gumā huā*
lotion (medical) - *marham*
lover - *āshiq* (U & mc); *prémī* (H)
low - *nīchā*
lunch - *dopehar kā khānā*

M

market - *bāzār*
marriage - *shādī*
mask - *maqūb* (U); *mukhauṭā* (H)
mat - *chaṭāī*
matches - *māchis*
material - *sāmān*
meaning - *matlab*
medicine - *davāī*
melt - *pighalnā*
message - *sandésh* (H & mc); *paigām* (U)
milk - *dūdh*
minute (time) - *minaṭ*
minute (small) - *bahut chhoṭā*
mirror (n) - *āīnā; shīshā* (colloquial)
money - *paisā*
monkey - *bandar*
monsoon - *barsāt*

month - *mahīnā*
more - *zyādā*
mosquito - *machchhar*
mosquito net - *machchhar dānī*
mostly - *zyādātar*
mother - *mā*
motor cycle - *motar saikil; phaṭphaṭiyā* (colloquial)
much - *bahut*
museum - *ajāyab ghar*
Muslim - *mussalmān; muslim*

N

name - *nām*
narrow - *tañg*
nationality - *qaumiat* (U); *rāshṭrīyatā* (H)
near - *nazdīk*
necessary - *zurūrī*
needle (n) - *suī*
neighbour - *paṛosī*
new - *nayā* (m); *naī* (f)
newspaper - *akhbār*
next - *aglā*
nice - *achchhā*
night - *rāt*
noise - *shor*
north - *uttar* (H & mc); *shumāl*
nose - *nāk*
notebook - *kapī*
now - *ab*
nurse (n) - *nars*

O

oath - *kasam* (U); *shapath* (H)
occupation - *kām; dhandhā*
old (thing) - *purānā*
old (person) - *būṛhā*
only (one and) - *vāhid* (U); *ékmātr* (H)
only (only he) - *sirf*
open (adj) - *khulā*
open (v) - *kholnā*
opium - *afīm*
order (n) - *hukam*
order (v - not for food) - *hukam dénā*
order for food - *khāné kā orḍar*
outdoors (in open spaces) - *khulé ilākoñ méñ*
outside/outdoors - *bāhar*

P

pain (n) - *dard*
painting(s) - *tasvīr(éñ)*
parcel (n) - *pārsal*
parents - *mābāp*
park - *pārk*
pearl - *motī*
pharmacy - *davāī kī dukān*
photograph (n) - *foṭo; tasvīr*
pickpocket - *jéb katrā*
piece - *ṭukṛā*
plan (n) - *mansūbā* (U); *yojnā* (H)
plate - *pléṭ; tashtarī*
pleasant - *suhānā*
pocket - *jéb*
poetry - *shāyarī* (U); *kavitā* (H)

poison (n) - *zehar*
poisonous - *zehrīlā*
postage - *ḍāk ṭikaṭ*
postcard - *posṭkārḍ*
post office - *ḍāk khānā*
prefer (v) - *pasand karnā*
pregnant - *ummīd sé* (expecting)
prescription - *nuskhā; priskripshan*
prevent - *roknā*
prohibit - *manā karnā*
prostitute - *tavāyaf* (U); *véshyā* (H); *ranḍī* (mc)
puppet(s) - *kaṭhputlī(yāñ)*

Q

quality - *gun* (H); *tāsīr* (U)
quantity - *tādād* (U & mc); *mātrā* (H)
quiet - *khāmosh*
quilt - *razāī* (mc); *lihāf*
quinine - *kwinīn*

R

really - *vākaī*
red - *lāl*
refrigerator - *frij*
refund (v) - *paisé vāpis karnā*
region - *ilākā*
religion - *mazhab* (U & mc); *dharm* (H)
rent (n) - *kirāyā*
reservation (v) - *rezarvéshan; buk karnā*
rich - *amīr*
right (hand) - *dāhinā; dāyéñ*
right(s) (of people, etc) - *haq(ūq)*

river - *nadī*
roof - *chhat*
room - *kamrā*
rope - *rassī*
rotten - *galā huā; saṛā huā*
rough (surface) - *khurdurā*
round (circular) - *gol*
round (of drinks/food, etc) - *daur*
rub (v) - *malnā*
rubber (material/eraser) - *rabaṛ*

S

sacred - *pavitr* (H); *muqaddas* (U)
salt - *namak*
salty; savouries - *namkīn*
sand - *rét*
sandals - *saiṇḍal*
school - *skūl* (mc); *madarsā* (U); *vidyālay* (H)
sea - *samundar*
seat (n) - *sīṭ; kursī*
seat belt - *kursi kī péṭī*
second (2nd) - *dūsrā*
second (unit of time) - *sekanḍ*
section (portion) - *hissā*
sell - *béchnā*
send (v) - *bhéjnā*
servant - *naukar*
several - *kaī*
sew (v) - *sīnā*
shave (v) - *hajāmat*
shell(s) (from the sea) - *sīpī(yāñ)*
ship - *kishtī*

shiver – *kāñpnā*
shoe – *jūtā*
shoe laces – *tasmé*
shop – *dukān*
short (height) – *chhoṭā*
short (less) – *kam*
shortcut – *chhoṭā rāstā*
shout (v) – *chillānā*
signature – *dastkhat*
silent – *khāmosh*
silver – *chāndī*
similar – *usī tarah kā*
since – *-sé*
singer – *gāné wālā*
sit (v) – *baiṭhnā*
size – *sāiz; māp; nāp*
sleep (v) – *sonā*
sleep (n) – *nīñd*
small – *chhoṭā*
smell (v) – *sūñghnā*
smile – *muskān*
snake – *sāñp*
soap – *sābun*
soft (texture) – *mulāyam*
soiled – *mailā*
solid – *ṭhos*
sorry (he is . . .) – *sharmindā*
sorry! (excuse me!) – *māf kījiyé*
soul – *rūh* (U); *ātmā* (H)
sour – *khaṭṭā*
south – *junūb; dakshin* (mc)
speed – *tézī*

spicy - *masālédār*
spit/sputum (n & v) - *thūk*
spoil - *khārāb karnā*
spoon (also 'sycophant') - *chammach; chamchā*
stamp - *ṭikaṭ*
steal (v) - *churānā*
stomach - *péṭ*
stomachache - *péṭ dard*
stone (n) - *patthar*
stop (v) - *roknā*
stop (n) bus- - *sṭāp; sṭop*
strange - *ajīb*
street - *saṛak*
student - *paṛhné wālā*
style - *ḍhang*
sunshine - *dhūp*
sweat (n) - *pasīnā*
sweet (adj) - *mīṭhā*
sweet(s) (n) - *miṭhāī*
swim (v) - *tairnā*

T

table - *méz*
tablet (medicine) - *ġolī*
tailor - *darzī*
take off (clothes) - *utārnā*
tax - *ṭaiks; kar* (H)
tea - *chāy*
teacher - *māsṭar; paṛhāné wālā; ustād*
tear (v) - *phāṛnā*
telegram - *tār*
television - *ṭélīvizyon; dūrdarshan* (India only)

tent – *tambū*
theatre (play) – *nāṭak; ḍrāmā*
theatre (the building) – *rangmanch* (H); *théṭar*
these/this – *yé*
thick – *moṭā*
thin – *patlā*
thought – *khayal*
thread – *dhāgā*
ticket – *ṭikaṭ*
tiger – *chītā*
timetable – *ṭāim ṭébl*
tiresome – *thakané wālā*
today – *āj*
toilet (make-up) – *sringār*
toilet (lavatory) – *pākhānā* (U); *shauchālayā* (H)
tomorrow – *kal; āné wālā*
tool – *auzār;*
tooth – *dāṅt*
toothbrush – *brash; burush*
torch (electric) – *ṭorch; baiṭarī*
torch (fire) – *mashāl*
total – *kul*
touch (v) – *chhūnā*
tourist – *paryaṭak* (H)
towel – *taulīyā*
train – *rél gāṛī*
translation – *tarjumā* (U); *anuvād* (H)
treatment (medicine) – *īlāj*
tree – *péṛ*
truck – *ṭrak*
type (kind; sort) – *qism*
typhoid – *haizā*

U

umbrella - *chhatrī*
understand? (did you . . .) - *samjhé (m); samjhī (f)*
underwear (briefs) - *kachchhā*
unripe - *kachchā*
unusual - *ajīb o garīb*
urinate - *péshāb karnā*
useful - *fāyadé mand*

V

vacation - *chhuṭṭī*
vegetarian - *sabzīkhor* (U); *shākāhārī* (H)
village - *gāoñ*
vomit (v) - *ulṭī karnā*

W

wait - *intézār*
wake (up)! - *jāgo!*
want - *zurūrat*
warm - *garam*
wash (v) - *dhonā*
waste (v) - *zāyā karnā*
watch (n) - *gharī*
water - *pānī*
waterfall - *jharnā*
waves - *lehréñ*
wax - *mom*
week - *haftā*
well (water) - *kūāñ; bāolī*
west - *pashchim* (H & mc); *magrib* (U)
wheel - *pahīyā*
whistle - *sīṭī*

white - *suféd*
whole - *pūrā; sārā*
wide - *chauṛā*
wife - *bībī, bīvī*
within (something) - *méñ*
within (inside) - *andar*
wood - *lakṛī*
work - *kām*
worship - *pūjā* (H); *ibādat* (U)
wrap up - *lapéṭnā*
writer - *likhné wālā*
writing paper - *likhné kā kāgaz*

X

xerox - *zīroks; foṭokopī; foṭosṭaiṭ*

Y

year - *sāl*
yellow - *pīlā*
yesterday - *kal; bītā huā kal*

Z

zoo - *zū; chiṛīyā ghar*

Language Survival Kits

Arabic (Egyptian) phrasebook

Arabic (Moroccan) phrasebook

Brazilian phrasebook

Burmese phrasebook

Eastern Europe phrasebook
Covers Bulgarian, Czech, Hungarian, Polish, Romanian and Slovak.

Thai Hill Tribes phrasebook

Hindi/Urdu phrasebook

Indonesian phrasebook

Japanese phrasebook

Korean phrasebook

Mandarin Chinese phrasebook

Mediterranean Europe phrasebook
Covers Albanian, Greek, Italian, Macedonian, Maltese, Serbian & Croatian and Slovene.

Nepali phrasebook

Pidgin phrasebook

Pilipino phrasebook

Quechua phrasebook

Russian phrasebook

Scandinavian Europe phrasebook
Includes the following: Danish, Finnish, Icelandic, Norwegian and Swedish.

Spanish (Latin American) phrasebook

Sri Lanka phrasebook

Swahili phrasebook

Thai phrasebook

Tibet phrasebook

Turkish phrasebook

Vietnamese phrasebook

Western Europe phrasebook
Useful words and phrases in Basque, Catalan, Dutch, French, German, Irish, Portuguese, Spanish (Castilian).

LONELY PLANET PUBLICATIONS
Australia: PO Box 617, Hawthorn, Victoria 3122
USA: 155 Filbert Street, Suite 251, Oakland CA 94607-2538
UK: 12 Barley Mow Passage, Chiswick, London W4 4PH

Keep in touch!

We love hearing from you and think you'd like to hear from us.

The Lonely Planet newsletter covers the when, where, how and what of travel. (AND it's free!)

***When**...is the right time to see reindeer in Finland?*
***Where**...can you hear the best palm-wine music in Ghana?*
***How**...do you get from Asunción to Areguá by steam train?*
***What**...should you leave behind to avoid hassles with customs in Iran?*

To join our mailing list just contact us at any of our offices. (details below)

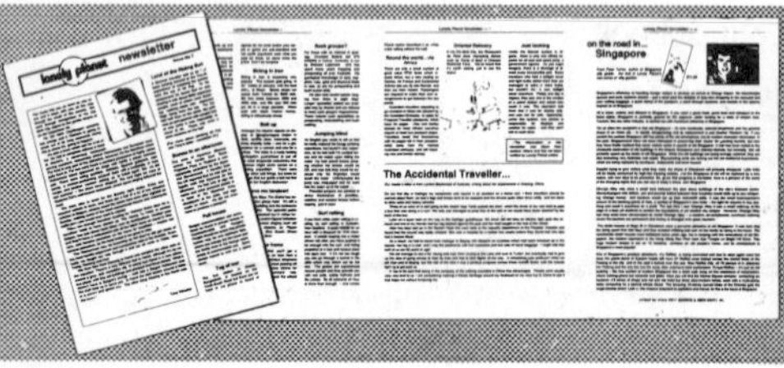

Every issue includes:

- *a letter from Lonely Planet founders Tony and Maureen Wheeler*
- *travel diary from a Lonely Planet author - find out what it's really like out on the road*
- *feature article on an important and topical travel issue*
- *a selection of recent letters from our readers*
- *the latest travel news from all over the world*
- *details on Lonely Planet's new and forthcoming releases*

Also available Lonely Planet T-Shirts. 100% heavy weight cotton (S, M, L, XL)

LONELY PLANET PUBLICATIONS
Australia: PO Box 617, Hawthorn, Victoria 3122 (tel: 03-819 1877)
USA: 155 Filbert Street, Suite 251, Oakland, CA 94607 (tel: 510-893 8555)
UK: 12 Barley Mow Passage, Chiswick, London W4 4PH (tel: 081-742 3161)